FUN
FACTS
for
Baseball
Fans

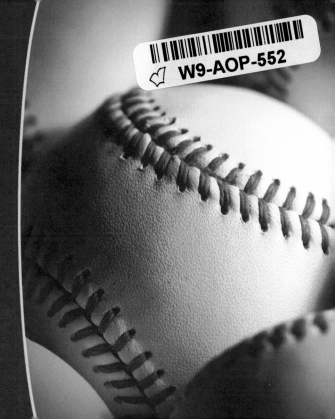

© 2010 by Barbour Publishing, Inc.

Written and compiled by Paul Kent.

ISBN 978-1-60260-714-9

Published by Barbour Publishing, Inc., P.O. Box 719, Uhrichsville, Ohio 44683
www.barbourbooks.com

Our mission is to publish and distribute inspirational products offering exceptional value and biblical encouragement to the masses.

 Member of the
Evangelical Christian
Publishers Association

Printed in China.

FUN
FACTS
for
Baseball
Fans

BARBOUR
PUBLISHING

Introduction

What is it that makes baseball so popular—even beloved—among sports?

Maybe it's the long and storied history of the game. Maybe it's the combination of intense action and laid-back moments that make up every contest. Maybe it's the heroic young men who've entertained us through generations of play. Maybe it's the quirky lingo, the cool memorabilia, and the voluminous statistics of the sport. Maybe it's all of those things, and more.

Maybe, too, it's the way baseball just seems to reflect the human experience. There are so many parallels to be drawn between the game and who we are as people. With a little thought, we'll probably

uncover some memorable life lessons along the way.

That's what this book is all about. Consider this a box-seat ticket (for right behind home plate!) to the greatest game going. Read on for the first pitch of *Fun Facts for Baseball Fans*. . . .

1

The (Really Old) History of Baseball

1700: A minister in Maidstone, England, records his concern over people playing "baseball and cricketts and many other sports on the Lord's Day."

1778: An American revolutionary war soldier writes of a game of "base" played at Valley Forge.

1839: West Point cadet (and future Civil War general) Abner Doubleday supposedly invents baseball in his hometown of Cooperstown, New York.

Wherever and whenever the game of baseball began, the Bible is clear on the origins of everything else:

In the beginning God created the heavens and the earth.

GENESIS 1:1

1845: Modern baseball's first club, the New York Knickerbockers, is formed by Wall Street clerks and shopkeepers.

1846: Hoboken, New Jersey, hosts the first officially recorded baseball game, between the Knickerbockers and the "New York Club." New York is fined six cents for cursing—but still wins the game 23–1.

1858: For the first time, fans *pay* to watch baseball—in a best-of-three series between all-star teams from New York and Brooklyn.

1862: Baseball's first enclosed park—
Union Grounds—opens in Brooklyn.
Each spectator pays a dime to get in.

With an outfield wall, Union Grounds introduces a new element to the game: the over-the-fence home run.

1863–1865: During the Civil War, Northern soldiers introduce baseball to their counterparts from the South and West.

1869: The Cincinnati Red Stockings become baseball's first openly professional team. They'll win 57 straight games in a barnstorming tour before losing to the Brooklyn Atlantics.

1871: Baseball's first major league—the National Association—organizes with teams from New York City; Brooklyn; Philadelphia; Boston; Washington; Chicago; Cleveland; Fort Wayne, Indiana; Troy, New York; and Rockford, Illinois. In the very first game, Fort Wayne shuts out Cleveland 2–0.

1876: The modern National League—
with teams from Cincinnati;
New York; Chicago; Philadelphia;
Boston; St. Louis; Louisville, Kentucky;
and Hartford, Connecticut—begins play
as the National Association folds.

1901: The upstart American League claims major league status, directly competing with the National League in Boston, Philadelphia, and Chicago.

Friendly competition is great.
Just be sure to keep it friendly!

Do nothing out of selfish ambition
or vain conceit, but in humility consider
others better than yourselves.

PHILIPPIANS 2:3

2

You Can't Tell the TEAMS without a Scorecard

Professional baseball has had a total of seven "major leagues" since 1871.

The big leagues have included the National Association (1871–1875), the National League (1876–present), the American Association (1882–1891), the Union Association (1884), the Players League (1890), the American League (1901–present), and the Federal League (1914–1915).

American Association teams you might recognize: Brooklyn Dodgers, Cincinnati Reds, Pittsburgh Pirates, St. Louis Cardinals. Each ultimately switched over to the National League.

American Association teams you've probably *never* heard of: Brooklyn Gladiators, Cincinnati Kelly's Killers, Columbus Solons, Rochester Hop Bitters. (Huh?)

Union Association teams lost to history: Altoona Mountain City, Baltimore Monumentals, Pittsburgh Stogies, St. Louis Maroons, St. Paul Apostles, Wilmington Quick Steps.

Players League teams lost to history: Brooklyn Wards Wonders, Cleveland Infants, Pittsburgh Burghers.

Federal League teams lost to history:
Baltimore Terrapins, Brooklyn
Tip-Tops, Buffalo Buffeds (two
syllables: *Buf-Feds*), Chicago Whales,
Indianapolis Hoosiers, Kansas City
Packers, Newark Peps, Pittsburgh
Rebels, St. Louis Terriers.

Only a handful of baseball historians recall those short-lived teams of more than a century ago. But there are some things we should all keep fresh in our minds:

I will remember the deeds of the Lord; yes,
I will remember your miracles of long ago.

PSALM 77:11

The American League's inaugural lineup (1901): Baltimore Orioles, Boston Red Sox, Chicago White Sox, Cleveland Indians, Detroit Tigers, Milwaukee Brewers, Philadelphia Athletics, Washington Senators.

The Baltimore Orioles of 1901
moved to New York in 1902
to become the Yankees.

The Milwaukee Brewers of 1901 moved to St. Louis in 1902 to become the Browns. . .and in 1954 the Browns moved to Baltimore to become a new Orioles team.

A 1969 American League expansion team, the Seattle Pilots, moved to Milwaukee in 1970 to become a new Brewers team.

In 1998, the Brewers became the first modern major league team to change leagues—American to National.

That was one year after "interleague" play began—demolishing the wall that had long separated American and National teams during the regular season.

It's okay if you find all those changes a bit confusing. Know that the really important things *never* change.

Jesus Christ is the same yesterday and today and forever.

HEBREWS 13:8

3

A Little R & R
(Rules and Regulations)

The current 60 feet, 6 inch distance between the pitcher's rubber and home plate was settled in 1893. Before that, pitchers threw from the back line of a rectangular box, 55 feet, 6 inches from home plate.

Before that, pitchers threw from a six-foot-square box 45 feet from home plate—which was a 12-inch square of marble or other stone.

In the 1800s, bases on balls were awarded after anywhere from three to thirteen bad pitches. For a while in the nineteenth century, a batter was out after *four* strikes.

The four balls/three strikes ratio was settled—permanently—in 1889.

In baseball's early days, pitchers could throw from a running start or twist and turn to confuse batters and base runners as to where the throw would go.

The National League was first to allow overhand pitching in 1884.

Other rules oddities: At various times in baseball history. . .

. . .batters could be retired on a foul ball caught on the first bounce

. . .umpires had to wait until the end of an inning to replace a damaged ball

. . .teams could use fans—even in street clothes—as substitutes.

Baseball rules can and do change with time. . .but here's a (golden) rule that applies forever:

[Jesus said,] "In everything, do to others what you would have them do to you, for this sums up the Law and the Prophets."

MATTHEW 7:12

4

A Lexicon of Baseball Lingo

Apple, cowhide, horsehide, pill, potato, rock:
Slang terms for the baseball itself.

Bean:
The head, target of a "bean ball." Also,
as a verb, to hit an opposing player in
the head with a pitch.

Can of corn:
An easily caught fly ball. Term derives
from old-time grocers' practice of using
a pole to knock canned goods from a
high shelf, then catching the can
in the grocer's apron.

Cup of coffee:
A minor leaguer's brief visit to the
majors—because the rookie's stay is
usually just long enough for a hot drink.

Eephus:
A slow lob pitch with a high arch.
Origin unknown.

Goat:
A player accused of losing a game for his team. Probably a shortened form of *scapegoat*—though by definition a scapegoat is actually innocent.

Gopher ball:
A pitch that results in a home run.
Perhaps from the phrase "go fer"—as in,
"That pitch will go fer a home run."

Hot corner:
Third base. So named for the large
number of hard-hit balls to the
left side of the infield.

Keystone:
Second base. So named for the base's
position, as viewed from home plate, like
the keystone or crown of an arch.

Moxie:
Nerve shown by a ballplayer. From
an 1870s soft drink called *Moxie*,
advertised as a "nerve tonic."

Mustard:
Extra speed or power on a throw—
as in, "put a little mustard on it."
Also, what goes on those delicious
stadium hot dogs.

Pepper:
A warm-up exercise in which a batter rapidly taps balls to a line of fielders. "No Pepper" signs appear on many stadium walls today, to keep fans from being hit by errant balls.

Seeing-eye single:
A weakly hit ground ball that somehow gets through the infield for a hit. Also called a *scratch hit* or *bleeder.*

Texas Leaguer:
A weakly hit fly ball that falls safely between infielders and outfielders, also known as a *flare, blooper,* or *dying quail.* Name from a nineteenth-century Houston player who specialized in such hits.

A true fan knows the terminology of the game and uses it properly. How much better to use *all* our words correctly!

A word aptly spoken is like apples of gold in settings of silver.

PROVERBS 25:11

5

A Menagerie of
Baseball Monikers

Abbreviated "ing" nicknames:

"Hammerin' Hank" Aaron (1954–1976)

"Joltin' Joe" DiMaggio (1936–1951)

"Larrupin' Lou" Gehrig (1923–1939)

"Big" nicknames:

Mark "Big Mac" McGwire (1986–2001)

Randy "The Big Unit" Johnson (1988–)

Frank "The Big Hurt" Thomas
(1990–2008)

David "Big Papi" Ortiz (1997–)

Nicknames based on nationality
or birthplace:

Al Hrabosky, "The Mad Hungarian"
(1970–1982)

Juan Marichal, "The Dominican Dandy"
(1960–1975)

Ron Guidry, "Louisiana Lightnin'"
(1975–1988)

"Gettysburg Eddie" Plank (1901–1917)

Somewhat less obvious nicknames:

Denton True "Cy" Young (1890–1911.)
"Cy" is short for *Cyclone*.

Nicknames based on physical
appearance or qualities:

Mark "The Bird" Fidrych (1976–1980)

Harold "Pee Wee" Reese (1940–1958)

Mordecai "Three Finger" Brown
(1903–1916)

Walt "No Neck" Williams (1964–1975)

More nicknames based on physical appearance or qualities:

William Henry "Wee Willie" Keeler (1892–1910)

Ed "The Midget" Mensor (1912–1914)

William "Dummy" Hoy (1888–1902)
In less sensitive days, so called
for being deaf and mute.

Just plain weird nicknames:

Dick Stuart, "Dr. Strangeglove" (1958–1969) Spin-off of 1964 film *Dr. Strangelove*—so named for his poor fielding.

George "Highpockets" Kelly (1915–1932)

Harold "Pie" Traynor (1920–1937)

More just plain weird nicknames:

Odell "Bad News" Hale (1931–1941)

Benny "Earache" Meyer (1913–1925)

George "Doggie," "Foghorn," and/or
"Calliope" Miller (1884–1896)

Nicknames based on baseball achievements:

Lou "The Iron Horse" Gehrig (1923–1939) Played in 2,130 consecutive games.

Sal "The Barber" Maglie (1945–1958) Liked to pitch high and inside.

Pete "Charlie Hustle" Rose (1963–1986) Self-explanatory.

More nicknames based on baseball achievements:

"Tom Terrific" Seaver (1967–1986) Led the Mets to a World Series title in 1969—also known as "The Franchise."

Roger "The Rocket" Clemens (1984–2007) Threw hard for twenty-four seasons.

Reggie "Mr. October" Jackson (1967–1987) Elevated his already-very-good game at World Series time.

A good nickname carries value, highlighting a personal achievement, quality, or relationship. Jesus promises a new name to His followers:

I will write on him the name of my God and the name of the city of my God, the new Jerusalem. . . and I will also write on him my new name.

REVELATION 3:12

6

Great Milestones of Baseball

1903: In the first modern fall classic, the American League's Boston Americans (also known as the Red Sox) defeat the Pittsburgh Pirates in a best-of-nine World Series.

1919: With a .384 average, Detroit's Ty Cobb wins the last of his twelve batting titles. He'll hit .401 in 1922, but lose out to the Browns' "Gorgeous George" Sisler (.420).

1920: Babe Ruth nearly doubles the major league's single-season home run record by slamming 54. The Bambino had set the previous mark of 29 the year before.

1921: Ruth increases his home run record to 59—a mark that will stand for six years, until he swats 60 in 1927.

1921: In August, baseball hits the airwaves for the first time, as Pittsburgh station KDKA broadcasts a game between the Pirates and Phillies.

1923: On April 18, the famed Yankee Stadium opens its doors to the public. Construction crews built the facility in only 284 days.

1924: Rogers Hornsby of St. Louis records the National League's highest single-season batting average of the twentieth century, at .424.

Hornsby's mark is two points off the American League's twentieth-century best, Nap Lajoie's .426 for the Philadelphia Athletics in 1901.

1925: Cleveland shortstop Joe Sewell sets a big league record by striking out only four times in a full season—comprising 608 at bats. He'll hit .336 for the year.

Whatever you do, do as well as you can.

*Do you see a man skilled in his work?
He will serve before kings; he will
not serve before obscure men.*

PROVERBS 22:29

1927: The Yankees roll to one of the best seasons ever, posting a 110–44 record, winning the American League pennant by 19 games, and sweeping the Pittsburgh Pirates in the World Series.

For their overwhelming play, the '27 Yanks are immortalized as "Murderer's Row."

1930: The Cubs' Hack Wilson sets the all-time single-season RBI mark, knocking in 190. Along the way, he'll also set a long-standing National League home run mark of 56.

1933: Washington coach Nick Altrock pinch hits for the Senators—at the age of 57.

1934: Pitching brothers Dizzy and Daffy Dean win all four of the St. Louis Cardinals' World Series victories against the Detroit Tigers.

1939: The Baseball Hall of Fame and Museum is dedicated in Cooperstown, New York, with original inductees Babe Ruth, Ty Cobb, Honus Wagner, Christy Mathewson, and Walter Johnson.

1941: Reigning American League MVP Hank Greenberg leaves the Detroit Tigers to join the U.S. Army. Many of baseball's biggest stars will follow Greenberg into the American war effort.

You're never too big—
or too small—to serve.

Remind the people to be subject to
rulers and authorities, to be obedient,
to be ready to do whatever is good.

TITUS 3:1

1941: Two of baseball's more impressive achievements occur in the same season: Joe DiMaggio's 56-game hitting streak for the Yankees, and the .406 season of Boston slugger Ted Williams.

1944: The St. Louis Browns win the only American League pennant of their fifty-plus year history—and play the crosstown Cardinals in the World Series. The Nationals take the series in six games.

1947: Jackie Robinson breaks the major league "color barrier," becoming the first African American to play in the bigs in the twentieth century.

The Brooklyn Dodger first baseman will bat .297, steal 29 bases, lead his team to the National League pennant—and win the Rookie of the Year award.

1948: Negro League star Satchel Paige becomes a 42-year-old "rookie" with the Cleveland Indians. Paige will go 6–1 with a 2.48 ERA.

1952: Paige, now 46, leads the St. Louis Browns in wins (12), saves (10), and earned run average (3.07).

1953: The era of team relocation begins, as the Boston Braves move to Milwaukee. In 1954, the St. Louis Browns will become the Baltimore Orioles, and in 1955, the Philadelphia Athletics will move to Kansas City.

1958: Major league baseball reaches the west coast, as the Brooklyn Dodgers move to Los Angeles, and the New York Giants to San Francisco.

1961: Baseball's expansion era begins, with the American League adding teams in Los Angeles (the Angels) and Washington (a new Senators team, to replace the former Senators— who had moved to Minnesota to become the Twins).

1961: The major league schedule increases from 154 to 162 games. The Yankees' Roger Maris breaks Babe Ruth's single-season home run record, with 61—but his record carries an asterisk since it came in a longer season.

1965: Baseball moves "indoors," with the opening of the Houston Astrodome. The first game is an exhibition contest between the Astros and Yankees on April 9.

1965: Dodger pitcher Sandy Koufax throws a perfect game against the Chicago Cubs, his fourth no-hitter in as many years.

1965: Satchel Paige returns to the pitcher's mound. The right hander—now 59 years old—throws three scoreless innings for the Kansas City A's against Boston.

How do you think those 20-something Red Sox players felt after the ancient Paige shut them down?

"Rise in the presence of the aged, show respect for the elderly and revere your God."

Leviticus 19:32

1968: Detroit's Denny McLain becomes the first 30-game winner in 34 years, and the last one of the twentieth century, going 31–6 to win the Cy Young Award.

1969: Major league baseball goes international with the addition of the Montreal Expos to the National League. Other expansion teams in '69 include the San Diego Padres, the Kansas City Royals, and the Seattle Pilots. With 12 teams in each league, divisional play begins.

1971: The fourth game of the World Series—between Baltimore and Pittsburgh—is the first night game in series history.

1973: California's Nolan Ryan tosses two no-hitters in a single season—against the Royals on May 15 and against the Tigers on July 15. He's the fifth major leaguer to accomplish the feat.

1974: Hank Aaron eclipses Babe Ruth as career home run king, slamming his 715th against the Dodgers on April 8. Aaron will finish his career in 1976 with 755.

1977: The American League welcomes its first team outside the United States—the Toronto Blue Jays. The Seattle Mariners also join the AL expansion.

1980: The Philadelphia Phillies win the first World Series title in their 97-year history, downing the Kansas City Royals in six games.

1986: Boston's Roger Clemens strikes out a major-league record 20 batters in a 3–1 victory over the Seattle Mariners. He'll go on to win both the American League MVP and Cy Young awards.

1988: Orel Hershiser of Los Angeles sets a major league record by pitching 59 consecutive scoreless innings. He'll lead the Dodgers to a World Series championship, winning two complete games—and going 3-for-3 from the plate.

1988: Chicago's Wrigley Field becomes the last major league ballpark to install lights.

1992: The Toronto Blue Jays down Atlanta in six games to become the first World Series winner from outside the United States.

1993: Toronto wins its second consecutive World Series title, defeating Philadelphia on Joe Carter's three-run, walk-off home run in game six.

1994: Boston shortstop John Valentin turns an unassisted triple play and hits a home run—in the same inning.

1994: Due to a players' strike, there is no World Series—and no major league champion for the first time since 1869.

1995: Baltimore's Cal Ripken breaks the longstanding record of Lou Gehrig by playing in his 2,131ˢᵗ consecutive game. The streak will finally end in 1998, at 2,632.

Perseverance is a virtue!

Let us not become weary in doing good,
for at the proper time we will reap a
harvest if we do not give up.

GALATIANS 6:9

1997: The Florida Marlins become the youngest team to win a World Series championship, downing the Cleveland Indians in seven games. Florida had joined the National League as an expansion team only four years before.

1998: Mark McGwire and Sammy Sosa stage an epic home run contest, with the Cardinal first baseman finishing with 70, and the Cubs' outfielder with 66—obliterating Roger Maris's former mark of 61 from 37 years earlier.

1999: Boston's Tom "Flash" Gordon sets a major league record by recording his 54th save in 54 opportunities.

2000: The Chicago Cubs and New York Mets open the regular season with two games in Tokyo, Japan—the first regular-season games ever played outside North America.

2001: After the terrorist attacks of September 11, "God Bless America" replaces "Take Me Out to the Ball Game" as the seventh-inning stretch sing-along.

Don't wait for times of trouble before remembering God.

*Righteousness exalts a nation,
but sin is a disgrace to any people.*

PROVERBS 14:34

2001: The Seattle Mariners set a regular-season win record with 116— but fail to reach the World Series.

2001: San Francisco's Barry Bonds sets a new single-season home run mark with 73—but can't lead his team to the postseason.

2002: The Anaheim (formerly Los Angeles and California) Angels win the first World Series title in their 41-year history, a seven-game triumph over San Francisco.

2005: The Montreal Expos relocate to Washington DC to become the Nationals.

2006: San Diego Padres closer Trevor Hoffman saves his 479th game to surpass Lee Smith as baseball's all-time saves king.

2007: Barry Bonds hits home run number 756 off Washington's Mike Bacsik to surpass Hank Aaron as baseball's all-time long ball king.

It's great to be "king"—but always know there's one higher: Jesus Christ.

On his robe and on his thigh he has this name written: KING OF KINGS AND LORD OF LORDS.

REVELATION 19:16

7

Memorable Moments,
Great and Not-So-Great

1880: In a June 12 game, Lee Richmond of the Worcester Brown Stockings throws major league baseball's first perfect game.

Five days later, John "Monty" Ward of the Providence Grays throws the second.

1886: St. Louis Cardinals' pitcher Charlie Sweeney serves up a record seven home runs in a single game.

1899: The National League's Cleveland Spiders turn in the worst season of all time, finishing 20–134, *eighty-four games* out of first place.

1909: Cleveland Indians' shortstop Neal Ball turns the first unassisted triple play in major league history.

1920: Cleveland Indians' second baseman Bill Wambsganss turns the first (and so far, only) unassisted triple play in World Series history.

1921: George "Specs" Toporcer
of the St. Louis Cardinals becomes
the first major league position player
to play the game while (you guessed it)
wearing glasses.

1930: Babe Ruth earns $80,000 with the Yankees, $5,000 a year more than President Herbert Hoover. Ruth jokes, "I had a better year than he did."

1936: Pittsburgh Pirates' backup catcher Hal Finney has the majors' worst hitless season, going 0-for-35 at the plate.

We don't have to be stars to earn God's applause. In fact, He *knows* we're going to come up short!

He saved us, not because of righteous things we had done, but because of his mercy.

TITUS 3:5

1937: Cleveland right-hander Johnny Allen, with a perfect 15–0 record, loses the Indians' final game of the season against Detroit.

Allen, thinking his third baseman ("Bad News" Hale) should have stopped a hit that led to the game's only run, tried to pick a fight with his teammate after the game.

1939: In a September 24 game, the Boston Braves' Johnny Cooney—more than 18 years after his major league debut—hits his first home run.

The next day, Cooney will hit his second homer—accounting for all the long balls of his 20-year career.

1941: Brooklyn outfielder Pete Reiser is carried from the field on a stretcher after a beaning that prompts the Dodgers to experiment with plastic batting helmets.

1942: Brooklyn outfielder Pete Reiser fractures his skull running into the outfield wall.

1946: Brooklyn outfielder Pete Reiser breaks his ankle during a game.

Sometimes, you have to sacrifice for the cause.

I urge you, brothers, in view of God's mercy, to offer your bodies as living sacrifices, holy and pleasing to God—this is your spiritual act of worship.

ROMANS 12:1

1946: The New York Giants' Mel Ott becomes the first major league manager ejected from both games of a doubleheader.

1946: Brooklyn manager Leo "The Lip" Durocher says the crosstown Giants are "nice guys—they'll probably finish last."

Newspapers shorten Durocher's quote to the well-known maxim, "Nice guys finish last."

Finishing last actually has its benefits.

Jesus called the Twelve and said,
"If anyone wants to be first, he must be
the very last, and the servant of all."

MARK 9:35

1950: Cornelius Alexander McGillicuddy—better known as Connie Mack—retires after managing the Philadelphia Athletics for *50* years.

As a player and manager, Mack spent 61 years in major league baseball.

1951: The St. Louis Browns send a "little person"—3' 7" Eddie Gaedel—to bat against the Detroit Tigers.

Gaedel, wearing the number "1/8," earns a base on balls. . .and a ban from baseball officials who don't see the humor in the stunt.

1953: The St. Louis Browns' Bobo Holloman throws a no-hitter in his first major league start. He'll finish his rookie season 3–7. . .and never pitch in the majors again.

1958: Dave Philley, playing for—you guessed it—the Phillies, records eight consecutive pinch hits to end the season.

1958: Cleveland's Vic Power,
who steals three bases all season,
steals home twice in a single game.

1959: Against the Milwaukee Braves, Pittsburgh pitcher Harvey Haddix throws a perfect game through 12 innings. But he'll lose the game 1–0 after the Pirate defense fails him in the 13th.

1962: San Francisco pitcher Billy Pierce sets a major league record for most home wins without a loss, going 12–0 at Candlestick Park.

1962: Reigning American League batting champ Norm Cash, who'd hit .361 in 1961, slumps to .243—the biggest one-year drop ever for a batting leader.

1963: In the Houston Colt .45s' final game of the season, rookie John Paciorek debuts with three hits in three at bats, two walks, three RBIs, and four runs scored.

Hampered by injuries, Paciorek will never play another major league game.

1968: Late in the season, Minnesota's Cesar Tovar plays every position in a single game. While pitching, he strikes out future Hall of Famer Reggie Jackson.

1971: Montreal's Ron Hunt sets a major league single-season record by being hit by 50 pitches.

1975: The New York Mets' Joe Torre ties a major league record for futility, hitting into four double plays. Each time, he erases teammate Felix Millan, who had singled.

1975: Houston Astro Bob Watson scores the one millionth run in major league baseball history.

1979: Tigers' rookie pitcher Pat Underwood gets his first starting assignment—against his older brother Tom, of Toronto. Little brother wins a classic pitching duel, 1–0.

"Brotherly love" isn't just
for Philadelphia.

Make every effort to add to your faith goodness;
and to goodness, knowledge; and to knowledge,
self-control; and to self-control, perseverance;
and to perseverance, godliness; and to godliness,
brotherly kindness; and to brotherly kindness, love.

2 PETER 1:5–7

1979: Atlanta Braves' pitcher Phil Niekro leads the National League in wins with 21. But he'll also *lose* 20 games during the season.

1980: Minnie Minoso of the Chicago White Sox attempts an at bat at age 57—and plays major league baseball in his *fifth* different decade.

1982: Due to a quirky midgame trade, Joel Youngblood becomes the first major leaguer to get a hit for two different teams, in two cities, on the same day.

For the Mets, Youngblood rapped a bases-loaded single against the Cubs, learned he'd been traded to the Expos, and immediately caught a flight for his new team. In Philadelphia later that day, he was called in as a substitute and slapped another single.

1984: Kurt Bevacqua, who hit only 27 home runs in a 15-year major league career, knocks two over the fence for the Padres in the World Series against Detroit.

1984: Baltimore pitcher Jim Palmer retires after a 19-year major league career, never having allowed a grand slam home run.

1985: Duane Kuiper, a twelve-year veteran with Cleveland and San Francisco, retires with one career home run in 3,379 at bats.

2005: Andres Galarraga retires from the game one home run shy of the 400 mark.

2006: On Mother's Day, some of baseball's biggest stars—including Derek Jeter, Manny Ramirez, and David Ortiz—use pink bats. They were helping to raise awareness of breast cancer.

2006: Late-season call-up Kevin Kouzmanoff thrills Cleveland fans by hitting the first major league pitch he sees for a grand slam home run.

2007: Jarrod Saltalamacchia and Ramon Vazquez, the eight and nine hitters in the last-place Rangers' lineup, each hit two home runs and drive in seven in Texas's 30-run outburst against Baltimore.